Regaining Dominion

Margaret A. Sowemimo

Copyright © 2014

Margaret Adeola Sowemimo

All rights reserved. No part of this book may be reproduced in any form, except for the inclusion of brief quotations in a review, without the prior permission of the author in writing.

Unless otherwise noted, all scripture is taken from the New King James Version. Copyright © 1982 by Thomas Nelson, Inc. Used by permission. All rights reserved.

To order additional copies of this contact us:
Margaret Sowemimo
P.O. Box 800
Powder Springs, GA 30127
678-949-8883 or
www.chosenremnant.org
Email: margaretsowemimo@gmail.com

Amazon.com

Printed in the USA

ISBN # 978-0-9752974-1-4

Other book by the Author

TABLE OF CONTENTS

ACKNOWLEDGEMENTS ....

PREFACE ....

Chapter 1: **Man as the Creation of God** ....
Chapter 2: **Consequence of Satan's disobedience** ....
Chapter 3: **Disobedience of Adam and Eve** ....
Chapter 4: **Disobedience and its fruit** ....
Chapter 5: **The Seed** ....
Chapter 6 **The ministry of the Seed** ....
Chapter 7: **Dominion regained through the Seed** ....
Chapter 8: **Conclusion** ....
....

ACKNOWLEDGEMENT

I thank God for the role of my mother in my life as an encourager and intercessor. Your selfless sacrifice is well appreciated. We all love you!

I dedicate this book to My Savior and Lord, Jesus Christ. I walk in Victory today because of Your sacrifice.

Thank you for being The Lover of my soul!

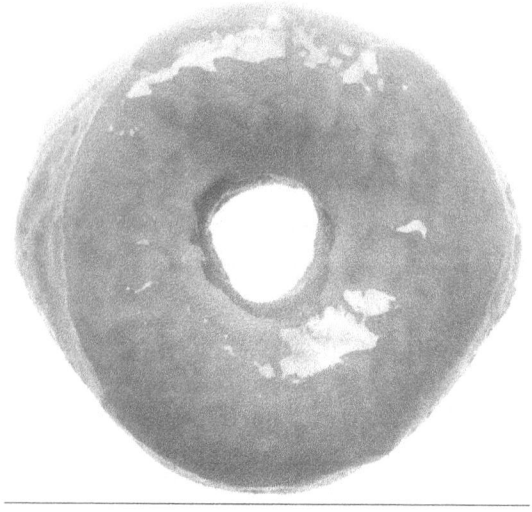

PREFACE

What does a donut have to do with regaining dominion? I believe you are acquainted with the hole in the donut. Man is born with a void in the heart which I liken to the hole in the donut. Satan also is aware of this void in the heart of a man without Christ. He capitalizes on this by trying to help fill the emptiness with things that afford temporal satisfaction.

All humans are born with a vacuum in the heart, which nothing in the world can satisfy. Some people believe if they attain certain status in life they will be satisfied. Some feel if they amass wealth or get married, they will be fine. After acquiring all of these, they still yearn for something more because the fissure remains.

Why do millionaires and celebrities commit suicide? Why are "people who have it all" miserable? The answer, the hole is still in the heart that no known surgery or material acquisitions can satiate. The only surgeon who can fix it is Dr. Jesus. He qualified to do this through His death and resurrection. Doctors of today pay the price with their time and money, but Jesus Christ paid the price with His blood (life).

Satisfaction for that longing can only come through a relationship with Jesus Christ. There are people who do not have much but are the most peaceful because of their relationship with Christ.

Money, fame, properties and other things will satisfy only for a time, and the yearning and longing will begin again. A day is coming when you are recognized not for the things you have acquired but for your relationship with Jesus Christ, the person who truly matters.

There is a Kingdom that is more real than the earth you live in. You can become part of that Kingdom today. The original plan of God was for us to rule, and reign but satan disrupted the plan. I have good news for you; the original plan can be restored in your life through Jesus Christ.

Take a journey with me to know where you are and where you can be. For those who are already Christians, we occasionally fall into self-rule, where we take control of our lives. If you are in such a place, retract, think of what needs to be changed and get back in right relationship with Jesus Christ.

An individual reading this book may say, "Jesus did nothing for me when I served Him. I am doing very well, now that I control my affairs. I am happier than I have ever been."
This is the deception of satan. You cannot find long-lasting happiness in the life you control. Christ is the center of true Joy.

A day is coming when the things you see and touch will no longer matter. Your name will be called, when the appointed time to leave the earth comes; whether you feel like it or not, you will respond to the call, meaning your eternity begins. You can freely accept His ruler-ship now rather than later after one dies. If after death, the destination is hell. There is no other way around it.

Joshua had perfect understanding that life is about serving the Lord in **Joshua 24:15**

> *"Choose you this day whom you will serve but as for me and my house, we will serve the Lord."*

I pray by the time you finish reading this book, you will have clear understanding of what Jesus Christ did for you, and you will no longer be the VICTIM but the VICTOR.

God bless you.

CHAPTER 1

Man as the Creation of God:

"In the beginning God created the heavens and the earth. .... Then God said, "Let Us make man in Our image, according to Our likeness; let them have dominion over the fish of the sea, over the birds of the air, and over the cattle, over all the earth and over every creeping thing that creeps on the earth." [27] So God created man in His own image; in the image of God He created him; male and female He created them."
Genesis 1: 1, 26-27

God created all things before man, but gave the authority to man. All of creation was to be in subjection to man. We were to rule and reign. God created man to look like Him and act like Him. Unfortunately, man kept God's image but lost His likeness because we inherited a sinful nature after the fall of Adam and Eve.

If I can reiterate, the original plan of God for us is to have "DOMINION" over everything He created.

Adam and Eve were one at creation because God said," let us create man . . ." He went further to say "let them"; man was singular, meaning though two individuals, but they were one. True unity in relationship today can only be attained as we submit back to the Lord as the sole ruler and possessor of our lives. Man could no longer govern the earth because of disobedience. HE no longer had dominion.

> *"Then God blessed them, and God said to them, "Be fruitful and multiply; fill the earth and subdue it; have dominion over the fish of the sea, over the birds of the air, and over every living thing that moves on the earth."*
>
> ***Genesis 1:28:***

God did not intend for man to labor so hard because at creation, God watered the plants through the mist that came from the ground. If Adam and Eve had stayed in His presence and obeyed the instruction giving, life would have been very easy and simple.

[5] Wild bushes and plants were not on the earth yet because the LORD God hadn't sent rain on the earth. Also, there was no one to farm the land.[6] Instead, underground water would come up from the earth and

water the entire surface of the ground.
Genesis 2:5-6 GW

The garden was a delightful place to live. Adam had such communion with God that He was asked to name the animals and whatever name Adam gave was the name the animal adopted. Some people view God as a dictator, if that was the case, He would not have given Adam the freedom to name the animals. He is still the same.

God did not create Adam a robot to be controlled, or He would not have asked Adam to name the animals. Adam at this time was in perfect union otherwise he could not have named the animals with such aptness. God was looking for a friend and He found one in Adam before the fall.

God came down in the evenings to fellowship with Adam and Eve. They did not have to search or try to find God, He always came to spend time with them. If man had just stayed within the parameter the Lord gave we would have had a perfect relationship with God.

> *Religion does everything by works, I need to do this and do that to earn God's favor but Relationship does everything by grace. I love because He first loved me. God favors me and enables me to please Him through the Spirit of Grace.*

Whether we want to accept it or not, we are born with the seed of evil in us because of the disobedience of Adam and Eve. A toddler can steal from the cookie jar and run to hide when he or she sees you coming, where did a child learn to know right from wrong; it is in each of us already at birth.

It is only redemption through the blood of Jesus Christ that can reverse our situation. If you claim to be a very good person and therefore do not need salvation, you are deceived. Isaiah 64:6 says:

> *"But we are all like an unclean thing, And all our righteousnesses are like filthy rags; We all fade as a leaf, And our iniquities, like the wind, Have taken us away."*
>
> ***Isaiah 64:6***

Genesis 1 recorded that the earth was without form and void and darkness covered the deep and the Spirit of the Lord moved, every time God spoke the Spirit of God moved and something was created. The Word of the Lord brought order out of chaos.

After the fall of Adam, man must confess with the mouth and believe in his/her heart that Jesus died and resurrected for their sin for the Spirit of God to move and bring about a restoration of the relationship with God.

CHAPTER 2

Consequence of Satan's disobedience:

Satan the father of lies;

We cannot fully comprehend this without throwing light on Satan and his intent to mar man the crown of God's creation.

> *"How you are fallen from heaven, O Lucifer, son of the morning! How you are cut down to the ground, You who weakened the nations!* [13] *For you have said in your heart: 'I will ascend into heaven, I will exalt my throne above the stars of God; I will also sit on the mount of the congregation On the farthest sides of the north;* [14] *I will ascend above the heights of the clouds, I will be like the Most High.'* [15] *Yet you shall be brought down to Sheol, to the lowest depths of the Pit.* [16] *"Those who see you will gaze at you, And consider you, saying: 'Is this the man who made the earth tremble, Who shook kingdoms,.."*
> **Isaiah 14:12-16**

The devil was removed from his position in heaven because of rebellion. He decided he would not go down alone. He made up his mind to pull man down from the place of perfection and wholeness that God had put him. This was his way of getting back at God for thrusting him out of heaven.

The pride of the place Satan found himself led to his rebellion. He believed because he occupied the positions of the worship and the covering cherub he could ascend to the throne of God to overthrow God. He forgot God is Omniscient (He sees all things) God already knew when He created Lucifer that one day he would rebel. God was prepared for that.

> *" You were in Eden, the garden of God; Every precious stone was your covering: The sardius, topaz, and diamond, Beryl, onyx, and jasper, Sapphire, turquoise, and emerald with gold. The workmanship of your timbrels and pipes Was prepared for you on the day you were created.* [14] *"You were the anointed cherub who covers; I established you; You*

> Pride is deceitful. It makes one think too highly of oneself. Because I see myself as very important, God will resist me. Pride keeps the focus on me, me and me. I see myself as the best and the one deserving of the greatest honor. "Pride goes before a fall, a lofty heart before destruction."

were on the holy mountain of God; You walked back and forth in the midst of fiery stones. ^{15} You were perfect in your ways from the day you were created, Till iniquity was found in you. ^{16} "By the abundance of your trading You became filled with violence within, And you sinned; Therefore I cast you as a profane thing Out of the mountain of God; And I destroyed you, O covering cherub, From the midst of the fiery stones. ^{17} "Your heart was lifted up because of your beauty; You corrupted your wisdom for the sake of your splendor; I cast you to the ground, I laid you before kings, That they might gaze at you. ^{18} "You defiled your sanctuaries By the multitude of your iniquities, By the iniquity of your trading; Therefore I brought fire from your midst; It devoured you, And I turned you to ashes upon the earth In the sight of all who saw you."

Ezekiel 28:13-18

Lucifer became haughty because he was created beautiful; his arrogance led to his downfall. The same creation he tried to destroy took over his position as the worship cherub. Man's position is now to worship God.

Ezekiel records that the devil was in Eden, he must have heard the instruction God gave to Adam and Eve. He also knew that God gave man a free will to choose between good and evil.

We must guard our hearts to avoid anything that could create pride in us. Whatever instruction God gives to us to abide by, is for our good. When we move away from it we run into problems that sometimes will have lasting consequences in our lives.

CHAPTER 3

Temptation and the Disobedience of Adam and Eve

> *"Then the LORD God took the man and put him in the garden of Eden to tend and keep it. ^{16} And the LORD God commanded the man, saying, "Of every tree of the garden you may freely eat; ^{17} "but of the tree of the knowledge of good and evil you shall not eat, for in the day that you eat of it you shall surely die."*
>
> ***Genesis 2:15-17***

There is a saying that "nothing good comes easy" but it can be easy if we always put ourselves in a place of obedience. God created all the beautiful things for Adam and Eve to enjoy but there was only one condition, they were never to eat of the tree of the knowledge of good and evil; for on the day they eat of it, they will surely die. Man had access to every tree in the garden **but one**.

I remember two of my brothers were extremely inquisitive. If any new electronic was bought by my parents, they are ready to dismantle it. A friend of my mother brought her a calculator with 110 volts. Our system used 220volts. Before the calculator could be used, there was the need to step it down. My mother warned us not to touch it but my brothers sneaked the calculator to their room, plugged it in the socket, and it blew. My brothers went into hiding because they knew they were in trouble and would be spanked. Their disobedience and curiosity caused my mum her calculator. The disobedience and curiosity of Adam and Eve caused us the fellowship with God and a life in the garden of Eden, which was a place of delight.

> *"1 Now the serpent was more cunning than any beast of the field which the LORD God had made. And he said to the woman, "Has God indeed said, 'You shall not eat of **every** tree of the garden'?" ² And the woman said to the serpent, "We may eat the fruit of the trees of the garden; ³ "but of the fruit of the tree which is in the midst of the garden, God has said, 'You shall not eat it, nor shall you touch it, lest you die. " ⁴ Then the serpent said to the*

woman, "You will not surely die. [5] *"For God knows that in the day you eat of it your eyes will be opened, and you will be like God, knowing good and evil."* [6] *So when the woman saw that the tree was **good for food**, that it was **pleasant to the eyes**, and a tree **desirable to make one wise**, she took of its fruit and ate. She also gave to her husband with her, and he ate."*

Genesis 3:1-6

The devil still uses the same tactics on us today as he did with Eve. The **lust of the flesh**, Eve saw that it was good for food. Eve was not starving; she had been eating before the devil showed up. She never noticed it was good for food until her attention was drawn to it. Obesity is a very common problem today in our society. I hear people say I know this is not good for me, but I will eat it anyway, and they gradually shorten their own lives. Eve knew it was not good, but her flesh could not resist the temptation.

Sometimes I know I need to go on a fast and the minute I decide to do it, hunger pang starts, my flesh cries out for food. It is in those moments that I see good food around me screaming "eat me, eat me."

Eve looked and it was **pleasant to the eyes,** this I will refer to as **the lust of the eye.** I believe the day God told them they could not eat it; He must have shown them the tree. It had no appeal to Eve until the devil came along and drew her attention to it.

> *The opposite of submission is to resist. When Adam and Eve obeyed the devil, they resisted God and submitted to the devil.*

People get into pornography today, because they took a second and third look at an inappropriate picture that was brought their way. Someone sees a neighbor's Mercedes Benz, and even though it is not something the person can afford; because it is appealing, it is purchased on credit. The interest rate may be so high that it becomes a point of stress for the person. However, because of the lust of the eyes, the person is now entrapped and has to find a way to pay the car note.

It is a tree to be desired to make one wise. Eve was walking in the cool of the day with the Father of Wisdom Himself so why did she think the fruit is what will make her wise. This is what we call **the pride of life**. She wanted to be wise in her own eyes. Adam named the animals without an input from God so obviously God had endowed them with great wisdom.

Earthly wisdom can do nothing to help us if we do not submit it to God, get counsel and directive from God. The wisdom of this world is foolishness to God. Majority of the times, worldly wisdom is about me and what will benefit me, not the people. Godly wisdom moves from self to what can be done to make a change. How can I impact someone else for God?

Solomon is referred to as the wisest man who ever lived. God gave him godly wisdom. He started off using it for the glory of God but later decided he was going to use his wisdom to secure himself and enlarge the empire. He moved totally away from God's counsel. He was not to marry foreign wives, or acquire horses from Egypt; he did all the things God instructed him not to. His disobedience cost him the Kingdom. He lost ten tribes to Jeroboam (Read the story in 1 Kings 11).

> *"But King Solomon loved many foreign women, as well as the daughter of Pharaoh: women of the Moabites, Ammonites, Edomites, Sidonians, and Hittites—² from the nations of whom the LORD had said to the children of Israel, "You shall not intermarry with them, nor they with you. Surely they will turn away your hearts after their gods." Solomon clung to these in love."*
>
> **1 Kings 11:1-4**

Adam and Eve had a perfect relationship with God until the devil showed up. The work of the devil is to steal, to kill and to destroy (John 10:10). He is always seeking to destroy the relationship that we have with the Lord. If we submit to God and resist him, he will flee from us. (James 4:7).

"Submission" is the ability to let go, believing you are secure in the care of another. It is giving up what you want for what the other requires or needs from you." I bring my own "sub-mission" under God's overall Mission. My focus is no more on what I want to achieve but on what God wants to achieve through me.

The opposite of submission is to resist. When Adam and Eve obeyed the devil, they resisted God and succumbed to the devil.

The devil knew what the Lord said to Adam and Eve; he operates in a way to entrap. The devil did not go straight to the point of saying, "did God say you should not eat of the tree of the knowledge of good and evil?" Instead, he said, *"Hath God said, ye shall not eat of **every tree** of the garden?"* If they do not eat of some of the trees of the garden how would they survive? He knew making an open-ended statement would engage Eve in a conversation. Eve fell for the trap, clarified God's instruction to the devil; it was not every tree but the tree of knowledge of good and evil is what God told them not to eat.

His trick is to lure you into a conversation. Getting you into a conversation allows him to mess with your mind. Eve was actually drawn into conversation with him. She went ahead to explain the instruction that God gave to them. You must never allow yourself to engage in any conversation with the devil because if you do, he will plant the seed of doubt in your mind, which may make you to question what you believe.

Maybe you are reading this book, and you have not accepted Jesus as your savior; the reason could be because the devil keeps deceiving you into thinking you are doing well without God. You are very successful; you have everything going for you, why do you need God to tell you what you can do and what you cannot do? Living independent of Him gives you the freedom to do whatever pleases you.

I have news for you, one day he will laugh at you, letting you know, you were foolish to have believed him. Do not let that be your story. Allow God to take the helm of your life, let God lead while you follow.

Christ came to rid us of the sinful nature. The offer of goat and ram could cover sin for a year, and you had to repeat the process again. The blood sacrifice was not going to be able to make us stand before a Holy God. God needed a perfect sacrifice without blemish. This is the reason the Son of God was chosen,

Jesus is the only qualify one. He shed His blood once, for all and the blood is still redeeming today. A person who lived 100 years ago received salvation through His blood and the person that will be born 50 years from now, if Jesus does not come before then, will need the same blood for redemption. This truly is something we cannot fully comprehend.

If you are a Christian, you must know the word of God. It is the only weapon with which we can defeat the enemy. The devil even tried to tempt Jesus in the wilderness after his forty day fast. This shows us the devil will do anything to thwart the plan of God. He considers himself very important, how can the created think he can overthrow the Creator? Satan is deceived to have thought he could overthrow God. He is still in the business of deceiving today.

He said to Jesus, "If you are the Son of God turn this stone into bread." Jesus at this time was hungry; Jesus had no doubt about whom He is. He did not need to proof His identity. He did not let the hunger situation distract Him from the real assignment. You must know your identity; otherwise, someone else will create one for you. satan deceives people into thinking the way you look and what you achieve are what make you the person you are.

Heaven does not need the things you accumulate here, why spend most of your life running around doing so many things so you can proof you are somebody. When we all come back with Jesus, He will give a new body, why do so many surgeries to keep your youth. There will come a time when you are too old to care. However, you can only rest in who you are if you full well know your identity is in Christ.

I did a message a while back on "Identity Crisis." The message was about people who do not know who they are. They dress well, have possessions but deep within are very insecure.

Sometimes in a gathering, you hear people boast of what they have or have achieved. They do that because they are insecure, they find their identity in what they possess not in who they are.

Eve could not comprehend the authority God had invested in them. She did not realize they are the crown of God's creation and the position they occupied made satan envious. She did not really understand their significance or she would not have listened to the lie of the devil.

God gave man dominion over everything He created. What position can be higher? God came down to fellowship with them in the evenings. They lacked nothing. Being overly ambitious is a dangerous thing. The ambition that led to the fall of Satan is the same ambition that drove them into succumbing to the lies of the devil; they want to be like God knowing "good and evil."

Satan deceived them into believing that, eating the fruit is what will make them somebody. However, they were already all; they could be in God.

The tree had always been in the center of the garden but Eve never looked at it before has been good for food until the devil made her focus on it. God said, "on the day, you eat it; you will surely die"; Satan says, "no you will not die you will only be like God." What had been of no attraction to her suddenly caught her attention?

"Godliness with contentment is great gain." Adam and Eve had it good in the Garden of Eden. Adam from godly knowledge named the animals. They could have anything they wanted if they had stayed within the boundary that God had set for them.

In the world today, knowledge is increasing at an alarming rate. However, the more knowledge increases the farther away some are going from the Lord, because they feel they have no need for God anymore. They possess the ability to run their lives.

> *Because of not knowing who you really are, you will settle for anything that will boost your ego or "seemly" do that.*

Some people in America are now fighting to take out "In God we trust" from the dollar. This shows how depraved the mind of man has become. The Nation was founded by the fore fathers trusting in God. Some people in the country now feel God is no longer needed in the running of the affairs of the country. We can see how far that has taken us, and it will not get better until we acknowledge God again.

Adam and Eve had a similar issue; they did not want to trust in God's ability to sustain them; they wanted to be like Him, so they know what to do and what not to do. They wanted to start making their own decisions.

I am the type of person that when something goes wrong, I can always find a solution. The Lord gave me a dream one day, in the dream; I had two horns on my head that I detested. My friends saw them as really cool, They envied me but I was very uncomfortable with them. There was a very tall man in blue suit in front of me; I did not see the face but I knew him in my heart as a friend. It seemed to me that we communicate a lot.

I knelt before him and said "Please take these horns away from me, I do not like them". He answered by saying, "Unless we take them away you cannot go to the next level in God. These horns represent your strength, your ability to get things done without consulting with the Lord."

I begged him to pray for me, and he did. I checked out the meaning of horn, and it stands for strength. I believe being strong is not the issue because God framed me that way but depending on my strength instead of him to channel my strength in the right direction is the issue.

Doing things in my natural ability has caused me a lot, and I look back today and thank God for the intervention through the dream.

Pride is what drives a person to want to do things without consulting with God. I repented before God. That dream has stuck with me. Can I truly say there are no more times that I try to run ahead of Him and do things, absolutely not, but I learn to check myself and when I do mess up, I quickly repent.

> *The LORD is my rock and my fortress and my deliverer; My God, my strength, in whom I will trust; My shield and the **horn** of my salvation, my stronghold.*
> ***Psalms 18:2***

In the above verse, He is the horn of my salvation, meaning He is my strength. The things I do, I do through Him because He strengthens me to do them. The horn is a symbol of strength and courage, but I needed to submit that to Him, so He can use for His own purpose.

I can no longer run ahead trying to use my strength to achieve things without consulting with Him. Some things are good but may not be what He wants for me.
The truth is, you cannot really experience the kind of life God wants for you without Him.

How many people died and at their funeral, had the accolade of man but are burning in hell now? Please do not be deceived you are either serving God, or you are serving the Satan; there is no in between.

Because Adam and Eve decided to eat the fruit, it caused them their relationship with God. They were alienated from Him.

When I was a child, my parents would tell us not to do certain things without letting us know why we should not to it. My brothers especially would go-ahead to do what we were told not to do. Majority of the times, attempting it ended in disaster.

I want to reiterate the calculator incident where my mom told my two younger brothers not to touch the new calculator someone just bought for her from the United States. My brothers enjoyed playing with electronics. They went behind my mum, took the calculator, and plugged it to see how it worked.

As soon as it was plugged into the socket it exploded. Both ran off because they knew what would follow from my mom. She told them not to touch the calculator but did not tell them the voltage from America is 110 – 120 v while Nigeria is 220 – 240 v. Their disobedience led to the destruction of the calculator as well as a good whooping from our mom. There is always a consequence for disobedience.

The devil convinced them that they will not die, their eyes will only open, and they will know "good and evil." They succumbed and ate the fruit, and their eyes were opened. They did not understand God was referring to spiritual death and not physical death.

Their disobedience led to spiritual death and the fall of man. God as a Spirit could no longer fellowship with man in his sinful state. Man was thrown out of the paradise of God, the Garden of Eden.

No matter, how good we think we are there are hidden motives and skeletons that may be in our cupboard that we do not want others to see or know about.

Why is it so easy to commit havoc in the night, it is because things can be hidden in the dark? It is the way a life without God is. The person is groping in the dark thinking they can see the light. What we call or see as light is actually darkness. God in His mercy has visited us to make Him known through Jesus Christ, so we no longer grope in darkness because we are now shown the way of peace.

> *[78] Through the tender mercy of our God, With which the Dayspring from on high has visited us; [79] To give light to those who sit in darkness and the shadow of death, To guide our feet into the way of peace."*
> **Luke 1:78-79**

> *[18] But the path of the just is like the shining sun,[a] That shines ever brighter unto the perfect day. [9] The way of the wicked is like darkness; They do not know what makes them*

stumble.
Proverbs 4:18-19

Before I surrendered my life to Jesus Christ, I saw myself as a very nice person. My African name is Adeola, meaning crown of wealth, a friend of my mother said I really should be called Adetutu, meaning crown is gentle. People noticed my gentleness.

The day I surrendered to Christ, I saw the ugly motives of my heart into things I did that I actually believed was done with good intentions. I will be honest with you; you are not capable of living right without being redeemed by the blood of Jesus Christ. If we were told to work for it or pay a great price for it, more people will want it because we are used to giving something to get something, BUT this is a free gift. You may wonder why it is referred to as "free." After all if something is called a gift, it should be free. We live in a world where most of the time what we call a gift has hidden demands later, or it is not fully free. Jesus came to redeem us with no attachment. There is nothing we have that He needs more than our hearts. Heaven does not need your possession. God is the Possessor of Heaven and Earth, why would we try to give back to God what is already His?

My mum shops a lot from magazines. At 83, she loves to see the word "free gift." It is all it takes for her to order something, even if she does not need it. She will purchase just so she can get her gift and later find someone to give her purchase to. The cost of the purchase is usually more than the gift which probably cost less than 50 cents and will be thrown away eventually. Most people like free gifts, no wonder we see the store do this type of advertisement a lot, buy one get one free.

The gift Christ has to offer is free and the only condition is you have to accept it. Your mom cannot accept on your behalf, and neither can you accept on behalf of your child. It is not like any other gift you can be offered. His gift is what determines whether you will spend eternity in heaven or hell. The rejection of it means eternity in hell.

You cannot choose how you want to serve God; you cannot obey in some areas and disobey in other areas. In the Old Testament, keeping nine of the commandments and sinning in one still made you guilty of all.

> *For whoever shall keep the whole law, and yet stumble in one point, he is guilty of all.*
> ***James 2:10***

Because I keep nine and someone else breaks all does not make me better than the person, before God we are both sinners. The same thing applies today, I cannot say I am serving God and still live the way I want to.

JESUS IS EITHER LORD OF EVERYTHING, OR HE IS NOT LORD AT ALL.

God gives an instruction concerning a situation, which is perfectly according to His Word, a friend, comes along to tell us it is not what God is trying to say, before we know it, we obey our friend and disobey God.

The devil always wants you to satisfy your flesh instead of the spirit, and it is a war we go through daily. The only way to overcome is to make up your mind that no matter the cost, you will obey the Word of God. We must cultivate the habit of prayer, worship and study of the Word daily.

There is a story in 1 Kings about a young prophet and an old prophet. God sent the young prophet on an assignment. He was instructed not to sleep in the town, neither was he to eat nor drink. An older prophet convinced him that **an angel** of the Lord appeared to him and told him the prophet could eat and drink.

The prophet obeyed the words supposedly given by an angel, disobeying the word given by the Lord. At the end of the day, the same-old prophet passed God's judgment on him for disobeying the word of the Lord. You can read the full story in 1 Kings 13:7-24

> *²³ For the wages of sin is death; but the gift of God is eternal life through Jesus Christ our Lord.*
> **Romans 6:23**

The word of the Lord above will one day prove true in your life based on the decision that you eventually make in this life.

When we have religion and not relationship, we are dead spiritually even though physically we are living. God is not interested in dead works.

God referred many times in His word, that the people are seeing, but they are blind, so it is possible to see and yet not see. Christ in the book of Revelation referred to the Church at Sardis has one that people saw as being alive but as far as Christ was concerned the Church was dead.

Without Christ, one is like someone on death row awaiting execution, and as he walks the hall way, someone pronounces, "dead man walking." This may seem harsh but the truth my dear one is without Christ one is dead even though in the natural eyes the person is living. **Keep reading and you will see the consequence of disobedience**.

CHAPTER 4

Disobedience and its fruit:

Adam and Eve because of disobedience lost the place of dominion. They lost the life in Eden where they had walked in perfect harmony with God. They lost the place of peace and provision. They now have to take care of their own needs. Adam will have to till the ground for their sustenance.

> " *"Then the eyes of both of them were opened, and they knew that they were naked; and they sewed fig leaves together and made themselves coverings. ^{8} And they heard the sound of the LORD God walking in the garden in the cool of the day, and Adam and his wife hid themselves from the presence of the LORD God among the trees of the garden. ^{9} Then the LORD God called to Adam and said to him, "Where are you?" ^{10} So he said, "I heard Your voice in the garden, and I was afraid because I was naked; and I hid myself." ^{11} And He said, "Who told you that you were naked? Have you eaten from*

> *the tree of which I commanded you that you should not eat?"*
> **Genesis 3:7-11**

God came to look for them; they were in hiding because their eyes had opened. They realized their nakedness, and Eve said to God "the enemy beguiled me." The devil is the father of lies, and he specializes in deceiving people. We must not be ignorant of his wiles.

Our disobedience to God's instruction brings shame. It exposes our nakedness. Adam could have refused to eat the fruit, but he ate it and instead of admitting his guilt, he laid the blame on the wife. We do that today, instead of admitting to our wrong; we pass the blame to someone else.

> [18] *"Come now, and let us reason together, "Says the LORD, "Though your sins are like scarlet, They shall be as white as snow; Though they are red like crimson, They shall be as wool.* [19] *If you are willing and obedient, You shall eat the good of the land;* **Isaiah 1:18-19**

When the devil wants to tempt you, he convinces you what you are about to do is okay by backing himself up with partial truth from the word of God or from things others are doing. Satan did the same with Eve. The minute you fall into his trap, condemnation sets in, and you realize it was nothing worth selling out for.

Adam and Eve tried to pass the blame one to another instead of accepting responsibility. We still do the same today, instead of admitting to the wrong, we pass the blame unto someone else.

> *When God is not in charge of your life, the blood of Jesus does not cover you and therefore you have no hedge of protection. The devil can mess with you and do whatever he likes. Christians who decides to dabble into sin will breach the hedge as well, unless they repent.*

"So the LORD God said to the serpent: "Because you have done this, You are cursed more than all cattle, And more than every beast of the field; On your belly you shall go, And you shall eat dust All the days of your life. [15] And I will put enmity Between you and the woman, And between your seed and her Seed; He

shall bruise your head, And you shall bruise His heel." [16] *To the woman He said: "I will greatly multiply your sorrow and your conception; In pain you shall bring forth children; Your desire shall be for your husband, And he shall rule over you."* [17] *Then to Adam He said, "Because you have heeded the voice of your wife, and have eaten from the tree of which I commanded you, saying, 'You shall not eat of it': "Cursed is the ground for your sake; In toil you shall eat of it All the days of your life.* [18] *Both thorns and thistles it shall bring forth for you, And you shall eat the herb of the field.* [19] *In the sweat of your face you shall eat bread Till you return to the ground, For out of it you were taken; For dust you are, And to dust you shall return."* [20] *And Adam called his wife's name Eve, because she was the mother of all living."*

Genesis 3:14-20

Due to their disobedience, Adam and Eve lost the harmonious life, the peace and the provision they enjoyed in the Garden and in its place; man has to toil to eat. The woman will suffer pain at child birth. Life of bliss was exchanged for life of pain. There would have been no death; losing loved ones would not have been in the picture at all.

Without a relationship with Christ, man remains alienated from God today. Someone once said to me "Christianity is a white man's religion." She said, "they only came to brain wash us," she, being an African American held on to the issue of racism and could not get pass that in her mind.

I did not contend with her, only told her if she wants to know if hell is real or not she can ask God to show her. God does not want to leave you in the dark if you do not believe in Him, but you must come with an open mind and a sincere heart to ask Him to make Himself real to you.

I told her to ask the Lord to make it known if heaven and hell were real. We did not communicate for about a year. The next time we communicated, she told me she was born again, I asked her what happened, she said one night, she dreamt she was on her way to hell and she woke up screaming. She said she literally felt hot when she woke up.

Because she went to the Lord with a sincere heart, the Lord removed her doubt. If you are one of those skeptics reading this, the fact that you have gotten this far means something is drawing you; it is the Spirit of God. Ask the Lord to make Himself real to you and I assure you; He will. I hope you are going to write me one day with your testimony, so I can rejoice with you.

Unto Adam also and to his wife did the LORD God make coats of skins, and clothed them. And the LORD God said, *"Behold, the man is become as one of us, to know good and evil: and now, lest he put forth his hand, and take also of the tree of life, and eat, and live forever."* Therefore the LORD God sent him forth from the Garden of Eden, to till the ground from whence he was taken. He placed at the east of the garden of Eden Cherubim, and a flaming sword which turned every way, to keep the way of the tree of life.

> *Thank God we do not have to work for salvation; we only have to believe in the finished work of Christ at the cross.*

God cursed the serpent because of this act of deception. He promised that the serpent would only bruise the heel of the seed, He will send to regain the dominion, and while the seed will bruise the head of the serpent (meaning the seed will take the Lordship back from him). God cursed the ground for the sake of Adam. The ground that brought forth fruit for man to eat became the ground that man will have to till before it can bear fruit. It is now through the sweat of man's brow that he would eat.

Eve will bear children with pain. Here are some other consequences of disobedience, sickness, pain, hurt, lack, death, sorrow, etc. Life will no longer be easy for man. Man has to work hard to enjoy the things of life. God sent them out of Eden; He put an angel to guard the place.

We praise God that He did not just leave man in his sinful state. God made provision for the redemption of mankind even before the fall of man because God knew man would fall. God's only son became the sacrificial lamb for the redemption of mankind.

This promise made by God in Genesis is what brings us to the New Testament. We will see how God fulfilled the promise made to Adam and Eve in the Garden of Eden.

I can rejoice because I have surrendered my life to Jesus Christ. I am once again victorious. I can live as God originally intended for me to, you can too. I trust that by the time you get through the book, you will also walk in victory as Jesus is allowed to become the Lord and Savior of your life.

If you are a Christian, who has been dillydallying, today is the day of salvation for you. It is time for you to regain your victory in Christ. We are in times that we cannot be one step in and one step out.

The devil is the accuser; he takes delight in finding reasons to accuse us. No matter what has happened in your life, the blood of Jesus can cleanse you from it. Your part is to accept that which has already been completed on your behalf.

These are the most common reasons I hear people tell me:

- For someone reading who feels he or she has no need for God it is probably because of one or more of these reasons. You are enjoying something in the flesh you do not want to let go. You are afraid God will demand you to let it go. The pleasure of this life is temporal but the life after is eternal. Choosing to reject Jesus here means you will rather enjoy now and suffer later, and the suffering will never end.

- Another may say I just enjoy the lifestyle I live even if I have to cheat and steal to keep this up. People do not know how I make the money; I just want to keep up the façade. I tell you, the day of reckoning is coming; you will pay dearly for that. You cannot cheat forever. You will be caught eventually, and if you do not repent and change your lifestyle, you will still end up facing God's wrath.

- Some other ones say they are trying to get their lives right before coming to the Lord. A question for you, how many times have you tried to do better but keep going back to the same thing you try to get away from?

  The reason is you cannot make yourself clean. Man does not have the ability to clean you up. The

power to change can only be yours
after you surrender to God and let
the blood of Jesus cleanse you.

The good news is no matter how far you
have gone; God can forgive you if you ask
and come to him. You may need to make
right some wrong but what would it profit a
man if he gains the world and loses his soul.
Dear one, life does not end here.

"I am trying to get my life right before I
come to the Lord."
"I now have to keep all these regulations
meaning I will no longer have any freedom."

These are things that the devil will use to
keep you entrapped. He knows you cannot
do it on your own, if it was possible, we will
not need a Savior

CHAPTER 5

The Seed:
The Birth of Christ:

"Then Joseph her husband, being a just man, and not wanting to make her a public example, was minded to put her away secretly. [20] But while he thought about these things, behold, an angel of the Lord appeared to him in a dream, saying, "Joseph, son of David, do not be afraid to take to you Mary your wife, for that which is conceived in her is of the Holy Spirit. [21] "And she will bring forth a Son, and you shall call His name JESUS, for He will save His people from their sins." [22] So all this was done that it might be fulfilled which was spoken by the Lord through the prophet, saying: [23] "Behold, the virgin shall be with child, and bear a Son, and they shall call His name Immanuel," which is translated, "God with us."
Matthew 1:19-23

When the fullness of time came God fulfilled the promise He made to Adam and Eve in the Garden of Eden. Mary a virgin was found to be with child. The Lord said "His name shall be called JESUS for He shall save His people from their sins."

The name God gave His Son made clear the purpose for His birth. He is the Redeemer that will fulfill the promise God made in Genesis 3. Christ is the seed that will bruise the head of the serpent (takes back the authority and regain the place of dominion for us).

> *[14] So the LORD God said to the serpent: "Because you have done this, You are cursed more than all cattle, And more than every beast of the field; On your belly you shall go, And you shall eat dust All the days of your life. [15] And I will put enmity Between you and the woman, And between your seed and her Seed;* ***He shall bruise your head, And you shall bruise His heel."***
> ***Genesis 3:14-15***

The fall of man led to the spiritual death of man, according to the warning the Lord gave to Adam and Eve in the garden, that on the day they eat of the tree of the knowledge of good and evil they will surely die.(Genesis

2:15-17). We inherited a sinful nature that only the blood of Jesus can cleanse. We lost fellowship with God because of the sinful nature. God as a Spirit could no longer commune with man who now was spiritually dead, even though still living physically.

> *If you are one who does not yet have a relationship with Christ, the ultimate goal of the devil is to take you to hell. You may think God is a loving God and He cannot send anyone to hell. God will not be the one sending you there; it will be you making that choice.*

In the Old Testament man was able to cover his sin by killing animals but it was not enough to take the sin away. God needed a perfect sacrifice, one without sin or blemish. The only one who qualified was the Son of God. Jesus is sinless because He is the second person of the Godhead who came in human form to deliver us.

- **Attempt to destroy the seed.**

Satan showed up again, in an attempt to kill the seed before He could fulfill the purpose for which He was born. He deceived himself into thinking he could outwit God a second time. God already knew what Adam and Even will do and had prepared redemption for mankind before it happened. The Bible says Jesus is the lamb slain before the foundation of the world.

> *"Blessed be the God and Father of our Lord Jesus Christ, who has blessed us with every spiritual blessing in the heavenly places in Christ, ^{4} just as He chose us in Him before the foundation of the world, that we should be holy and without blame before Him in love . . ."*
> **Ephesians 1:3 -4**

Learn something from here; the devil does not give up. He is a thief who has come "to steal, kill and to destroy" but we give God thanks that Jesus Christ came to give life and life more abundantly (John 10:10).

After the birth of Jesus, Herod working as an instrument of satan tried to kill him but failed. God protected the seed. Jesus grew up daily in stature, and in wisdom and the Lord was with Him.

When God takes charge of your life, He guides you in all that you do. The devil may try to derail you, but God will direct your path. The devil is not more powerful than God, and he can only go as far as God permits. God told satan when he tempted Job to try him in all areas, but his life was not to be touched.

This tells me that the devil cannot go beyond what God will permit if you surrender to the Lord. There is a hedge of protection that is around you, and unless there is an opening, the devil cannot do anything. The devil was only able to touch Job because the Lord permitted it.

> *"He who dwells in the secret place of the Most High Shall abide under the shadow of the Almighty."*
> ***Psalm 91:1***

When God is not in command of your life, the blood of Jesus does not cover you; therefore, you have no hedge of protection. The devil can mess with you and do whatever he likes. Christians who decide to dabble into sin will breach the hedge as well, unless they repent. If God has made a way for us to be forgiven why struggle with sin when Jesus has paid the price.

This is a word of encouragement for someone reading right now; if it seems like everything around you is caving in, do not take your eyes off of the Lord and what He has spoken to you because your victory is assured in the end.

For that one that still chooses a life of sin, remember "the wages of sin is death and the gift of God is eternal life." The choice is yours; enjoy what seems like heaven on earth now but what follows there after death cannot be compared to any pain you may have felt in this life.

God loves you so much; He wants you to spend eternity with Him. God's heart breaks when He sees us doing things our way. He does not take delight in sending anyone to hell. God has given us a free will; the choices we make determine where we spend eternity.

> *"That if you **confess** with your mouth the Lord Jesus and **believe** in your heart that God has raised Him from the dead, you will be saved."*
> ***Romans 10:9-10***

To **confess** means you are agreeing with another, in other words, agreeing with God that I am guilty as charged. To **believe** is to place confidence in God that the finished work of Christ is sufficient for you.

Our goodness without relationship with Christ is filthy before God. If you are still justifying why you do not need to have a relationship with Christ; read the account of Cornelius in the book of Acts, chapter 10. The scripture says he was **devout** and **one that feared God, gave alms** and **prayed to God always.**

The angel of God appeared to him in a vision to send for Peter. Peter came to tell him about Jesus and his need for salvation. If being a good person is enough, the angel of God would not have asked him to send for Peter. RELIGION IS NOT THE ANSWER; RELATIONSHIP IS THE KEY.

Paul said the things I want to do I do not do them. The things I hate to do are the things that I do. Who will deliver me . . .

[8] For I know that in me (that is, in my flesh) nothing good dwells; for to will is present with me, but how to perform what is good I do not find. [19] For the good that I will to do, I do not do; but the evil I will not to do, that I practice. [20] Now if I do what I will not to do, it is no longer I who do it, but sin that dwells in me. [21] I find then a law, that evil is present with me, the one who wills to do good. [22]

For I delight in the law of God according to the inward man. ²³ But I see another law in my members, warring against the law of my mind, and bringing me into captivity to the law of sin which is in my members. ²⁴ O wretched man that I am! Who will deliver me from this body of death? ²⁵ I thank God -- through Jesus Christ our Lord! So then, with the mind I myself serve the law of God, but with the flesh the law of sin.
Romans 7:18-25

Religion does everything by works; I need to do this and do that to earn God's favor, but relationship does everything by grace. I love God; He favors me and enables me to please Him through the Spirit of Grace.

CHAPTER 6

The Ministry of the Seed.

At age 30, Jesus began His ministry; the devil showed up again to tempt Jesus. He tried three times but failed each time.

> "*1* ***Then Jesus was led up by the Spirit into the wilderness*** *to be tempted by the devil.* *2* *And when He had fasted forty days and forty nights, afterward He was hungry.* *3* *Now when the tempter came to Him, he said,* ***"If You are the Son of God, command that these stones become bread."*** *4* *But He answered and said, "It is written, 'Man shall not live by bread alone, but by every word that proceeds from the mouth of God.'"* *5* *Then the devil took Him up into the holy city, set Him on the pinnacle of the temple,* *6* *and said to Him,* ***"If You are the Son of God, throw Yourself down.*** *For it is written: 'He shall give His angels charge over you,' and, 'In their hands they shall bear you up, Lest you dash your foot against a stone.'"* *7* *Jesus said to him, "It is written*

again, 'You shall not tempt the LORD your God.' "8 *Again,* **the devil took Him up on an exceedingly high mountain, and showed Him all the kingdoms of the world and their glory.** *⁹ And he said to Him, "All these things I will give You if You will fall down and worship me." ¹⁰ Then Jesus said to him, "Away with you, Satan! For it is written, 'You shall worship the LORD your God, and Him only you shall serve.'."*
Matthew 4:1-10

It was not the devil that led Jesus to the wilderness to be tempted it was the Spirit of God. Jesus had to conquer at every point that Adam and Eve failed. The devil tried to make Jesus walk contrary to the plan of God by challenging His divinity.

Adam and Eve succumbed to the temptation. They ate the fruit, thus satisfying the lust of their flesh.

Jesus overcame the lust of his flesh, although He was hungry. He told the devil, *"It is written, 'Man shall not live by bread alone, but by every word that proceeds from the mouth of God.'* "He used God's word to overcome.

Eve, on the other hand, doubted the word of the Lord but believed the word of the devil.

The devil asked Jesus to throw Himself down if He is the son of God. Jesus was not perturbed by the instruction; He could not be enticed by the offer. Adam and Eve, on the other hand, saw the fruit was good for food. Their eyes deceived them.

Jesus countered this offer with the Word of God. He had nothing to prove to the devil. He is the Son of God. He was not in doubt of that. Adam and Eve, on the other hand, were not confident of their position in God, or they would not have eaten the fruit from the tree of the knowledge of good and evil.

Now that you are saved, you have an identity in Christ. You have to be secured in your new-found identity, or you will continue to try to prove who you are and your ability to people, which can lead you astray. God loves you for who you are. He fashioned you the way you are. You are His child, and the devil cannot change that even though he tries. He whispers things to make you doubt your identity or doubt the freedom you now have in Christ.

> *² As far as the east is from the west,*
> *So far has He removed our*
> *transgressions from us.*
> **Psalm 103:12**

I see people who have accepted the Lord raise their hands from Sunday to Sunday when altar call is made. One of the reasons I believe for doing this is because they still do not have confidence in their salvation. They cannot believe that God has forgiven and chosen to forget.

This makes it easy for the enemy to bring condemnation in relation to our past. Jesus was very confident of His position, unlike Adam and Eve, who did not fully grasp their position in God!

Today knowledge is increasing but many issues still remain unresolved. With more worldly knowledge comes pride. Humans are trying to determine the course of their lives. Before God, what we call knowledge is foolishness. There is no way we can channel the course of our lives and find fulfillment.

What the world call success is not, when God is left out of it.

> *We know that we all have knowledge. Knowledge puffs up, but love edifies. ² And if anyone thinks that he knows anything, he knows nothing yet as he ought to know.*
> **1 Corinthians 8:1-2**

We see successful people commit suicide, why? It goes back to the hole in the heart of man that was created at the fall. We can find satisfaction in life if we surrender our lives to Jesus. We need to recognize we have sinned and ask for forgiveness.

Jesus after choosing His disciples trained them to do the work of the Kingdom. Jesus preached about the Kingdom of God, healed the sick, raised the dead and delivered the captives according to **Luke 4:18.**

> *"The Spirit of the Lord is upon me, because he hath anointed me to preach the gospel to the poor; he hath sent me to heal the brokenhearted, to preach deliverance to the captives, and recovering of sight to the blind, to*

> *set at liberty them that are bruised, to preach the acceptable year of the Lord."*

The book of **Acts10: 38** also tell us about His work; this sums up all that He did in ministry."

> *"How God anointed Jesus of Nazareth with the Holy Spirit and with power, who went about doing good and healing all who were oppressed by the devil, for God was with Him."*

Christ healed the sick. He raised the dead, and He set the captives free according to the above scripture. For your life and mine, He came to do the same. Apart from raising the ones who died in the natural, He came to give life back to the ones who are spiritually dead. He came to set us free from the bondage of the enemy. He made a public spectacle of the devil and triumphed over him.

The devil is not your friend. He can deceive a person into thinking they have it all made. He will make you believe you are doing very well because ultimately, he will demand the soul. He wants to populate hell.

During a meeting with an evangelist from India, she shared with us her encounter at a crusade in India. She said she had been preaching, telling the people what her God would do if they surrender their lives to Jesus.

One man with a monkey on his shoulder that he referred to as his god, challenged her. He said, "Tell me some things your God can do." She answered by saying, "He will give you life, peace joy, wealth, etc. The man said to her "my god has already given him all that, what else can your God do, that mine cannot? She said she was lost for words because when you look at these people, they have wealth and to him, wealth is it.

She said she asked the Lord to give her wisdom to answer the man's question. The Lord told her to raise her hand and pray this prayer, Lord; I want to be more like you. She did, the Lord then said to her "Tell the man to pray the same about his god." The man refused because he said how can I pray to become like a monkey?" She told the man, "If you cannot pray to be more like your god, why, then are you serving that god?

The man started to cry, and he gave his heart to the Lord. I see some people who carry around statutes they worship. How can you be the one carrying your god around or the one feeding your god? If the god you serve cannot carry you, you do not need to serve that god.

Satan entered into one of the disciples (Judas) so that he could betray Jesus. This was part of the plan and purpose of God to give the dominion back to man.
Judas did not realize he had become a tool to fulfill the plan of God.

God is not demanding a sacrifice from you before you can be saved. He just wants you to surrender your life, so He can be in command. It is when He is in control that you can fulfill His real purpose for your life.

When God fashioned you, He had a divine mandate on your life, let Him reveal that to you!

Satan thought he had won when Jesus hung on the tree, but even then. He could not take His life. Jesus released His Spirit to the Father at the cross; no one took His life from Him. Jesus finished the work; He started three years prior.

> *"And when Jesus had cried out with a loud voice, He said, "Father, 'into Your hands I commit My spirit.' " Having said this, He breathed His last.."*
> **Luke 23:46**

When Christ takes over your life, the devil can no longer hold you in bondage. You find liberty in him. If the devil tries to touch you, he will be messing with the apple of God's eyes.

Christians need to realize that we have Christ and the Spirit that raised Him from the dead lives in us. We do not just confess this, we must believe it. Some Christians spend more time fighting the devil that they have little or no time left to worship the Lord. If you are one of those, you need to refocus.

Should you give more time to the creature or to the Creator? If you spend more time in God's presence, you will not have to fight the devil so much. God fought the battle for the Children of Israel most of the time. Do not get me wrong, there are times you have to be in warfare, but if it is what you spend the majority of your time doing, you are taken away the time you could be worshiping the Lord. Jesus already defeated him and shamed him. He is in the best position to assist

Chapter 7

Dominion Regained through The Seed:

Immediately Jesus gave up the Spirit, the curtain of the temple was rent in two from top to bottom. The holy of holies opened to anyone that would repent and accept the atoning work of Christ. We no longer need a high priest to go in on our behalf; we now have access to God through Christ who became our High priest (before this time only the high priest could enter into the holy of holies and he had to purify himself before he could go in. If he did not, he would not come out alive.

> *"Having therefore, brethren, boldness to enter into the holiest by the blood of Jesus,"*
> **Hebrews 10:19**

The same privilege that Adam and Eve had in the beginning we now have, we can fellowship with God in the cool of the day, and we no longer need to hide ourselves or kill a goat or a ram to atone for our sins. Christ the perfect lamb became the sacrifice once and for all.

The stone was rolled away by an angel. When the disciples came to look for Him, He was no longer in the grave, only the grave clothes remained because He had no need for that anymore, He has become the Lord of life, death could not hold Him down, Hallelujah! He had bruised the head of the serpent in fulfillment of what God spoke in Genesis.

By the death and resurrection of Jesus Christ, we are redeemed from the curse in Genesis, because He became the curse for us. He took sickness, poverty, etc. upon Himself on the tree, so we can enjoy the blessings of Abraham.

> *^{13} Christ has redeemed us from the curse of the law, having become a curse for us for it written*
>
> *"Cursed is everyone who hangs on a tree"*
>
> **Galatians 3:13**

Some people feel that God has changed and He is now a very simple God, well in a way I will say "yes" because we do not have to keep killing animals to cover our sins or receive the kind of instant judgment that the children of Israel received. But that still does not mean God no longer judges sin. Living in a time of grace does not mean we continue to live in sin. The book of Romans 6:1-2 says:

"What shall we say then? Shall we continue in sin, that grace may abound?
God forbid. How shall we, that are dead to sin, live any longer therein?"

We either choose to serve God or serve the devil, there is no in-between. Hell is not a place for man. God meant it for the devil and his angels. I pray that you will make the right choice in serving the ONE and ONLY TRUE GOD.

Many people saw Him after the resurrection. He stayed with the apostles for forty days.

> *"Then the eleven disciples went away into Galilee, to the mountain which Jesus had appointed for them. [17] When they saw Him, they worshiped Him; but some doubted. [18] And Jesus came and spoke to them, saying, "All authority has been given to Me in heaven and on earth.*

[19] "Go therefore and make disciples of all the nations, baptizing them in the name of the Father and of the Son and of the Holy Spirit, [20] "teaching them to observe all things that I have commanded you; and lo, I am with you always, even to the end of the age." Amen."
Matthew 28:16-20

"Later He appeared to the eleven as they sat at the table; and He rebuked their unbelief and hardness of heart, because they did not believe those who had seen Him after He had risen. [15] And He said to them, "Go into all the world and preach the gospel to every creature. [16] "He who believes and is baptized will be saved; but he who does not believe will be condemned. [17] "And these signs will follow those who believe: In My name they will cast out demons; they will speak with new tongues; [18] "they will take up serpents; and if they drink anything deadly, it will by no means hurt them; they will lay hands on the sick, and they will recover."."

Mark 16:14-18

Jesus before his departure gave all authority to the disciples and everyone who would repent and be baptized would be saved. We are now back to the place of DOMINION like in the beginning. We have authority over sickness, demons and all the power of the enemy as Jesus promised before leaving.

> *We are created to master life and not life master us. Freedom without a boundary is bondage. God gives us boundaries for our protection.*

The sad thing is some of us still walk in defeat. We walk around the way Adam and Eve did when they were thrown out of the Garden of Eden. The devil looks at us and laughs, because he knows we do that because we have not come to the realization that he has been defeated; and has no more power over us. The devil can only win the battles that you allow him to win in your life.

THE DEVIL IS NOW SUBJECT TO YOU BECAUSE YOU HAVE DOMINION ONCE AGAIN!

In the book of Philippians we see how God has highly exalted Jesus Christ and given Him a name which is above every other name. At the name of Jesus, every knee has to bow, the devil and his demons inclusive. Do not be afraid of the devil, be fearful of God. If we are obedient, we shall eat the good of the Land. We can open the door for the enemy to harass us if we walk in disobedience. May God give us the grace to be obedient at all times in Jesus name!

> *"Therefore God also has highly exalted Him and given Him the name which is above every name, that at the name of Jesus every knee should bow, of those in heaven, and of those on earth, and of those under the earth, [11] and that every tongue should confess that Jesus Christ is Lord, to the glory of God the Father.;"*
>
> **Philippians 2:9-11**

CONCLUSION:

After we are saved, if we sin, we have an advocate with the Father the man Christ Jesus. We can go before God, confess and repent of the sin and God will forgive. The worst mistake we can make is to stand before God and try to justify our position. We must humble ourselves and allow God to deal with issues in our lives.

It is only the knowledge of the truth that can make us free. **Jesus Christ** is the **TRUTH,** and if we allow Him to lead us; we will be okay. We were created to master life not life master us. Freedom without a boundary is bondage. God gives us boundaries for our protection.

The first Adam in relationship with God was to populate the earth and dominate it, but he failed in that assignment.

Jesus came as the second and last Adam to populate the Kingdom and restore our place of dominion. He succeeded in His assignment. He leaves me a choice in the acceptance of the finished work.

Adam and Eve had a choice of serving God by obeying Him but they failed. Today you have a choice also, you can accept the finished work of redemption in Christ by acknowledging you are a sinner and allow Him to take over the ruler-ship of your life.

Adam and Eve chose self-rule instead of God-rule. What would be your choice today?

Someone reading may wonder "Why did God put the tree of the knowledge of good and evil in the garden when He knew Adam and Eve will fall to the temptation of eating from the tree?"

How would you feel if someone claims to love you, but you have to force the person to show it?

God loved Adam and Eve very much that He gave them a free will to take decisions. He brought the animals to Adam in Genesis to name; He had no input in the choice of names given. He told them to keep away from the tree as well as what the consequence of disobedience would be. They doubted His love by doing exactly what He told them not to do.

Choosing to ignore the redemptive work of Christ will eventually lead to death; eternal separation from God. Adam and Eve knew what God said; they lived with the consequence of their disobedience. We inherited that from them.
Thank God for Christ, who came to set us free!
You can choose life right now.

If you have decided to give Jesus your heart, pray this prayer:

Father in the name of Jesus Christ I come to you today and ask you to forgive me of all my sins. I repent and turn away from them. I ask that you will help me not to go back to a life of sin. Jesus I confess you as the Lord of my life today.

The Word of God in "***Romans 10:9-10*** says

> *"That if you confess with your mouth the Lord Jesus and believe in your heart that God has raised Him from the dead, you will be saved. ^{10} For with the heart one believes unto righteousness, and with the mouth confession is made unto salvation."*

I have confessed you with my mouth, and I believe in my heart that God raised you from the dead. I am therefore saved and have become a new creation.

As new covenant believers, we are not to labor in our strength for the expansion of the Kingdom of God. We are to rely on the leading of the Holy Spirit. God expected Adam and Eve to rely on Him. Our union with God requires us to be fruitful, just as He expected Adam and Eve to have been.

Jesus in **Matthew 28:19** told the disciples also to be fruitful.

> "Go therefore[a] and make disciples of all the nations, baptizing them in the name of the Father and of the Son and of the Holy Spirit..."

Adam was to be fruitful and multiply, replenish the earth and subdue it. The first Adam was to populate the earthly kingdom. The last Adam came to populate The Heavenly Kingdom. (Thy Kingdom come, thy will be done on earth as it is in heaven). Communion between Adam and Eve was to produce natural children while communion between Christ and His Church is to produce spiritual children. As the bride of Christ we are also required to be fruitful and to multiply. Evidence of life is growth.

We will one day reign with Him in the new earth. There will be no more sorrow, sickness and pain.

> ^{12} looking for and hastening the coming of the day of God, because of which the heavens will be dissolved, being on fire and the elements will melt with fervent heat? ^{13} Nevertheless we, according to His promise, look for new heavens and a new

earth in which righteousness dwells. ¹⁴ Therefore, beloved, looking forward to these things, be diligent to be found by Him in peace, without spot and blameless
2 Peter 3:12-14

21 Now I saw a new heaven and a new earth, for the first heaven and the first earth had passed away. Also there was no more sea. ² Then I, John,⁽ᵃ⁾ saw the holy city, New Jerusalem, coming down out of heaven from God, prepared as a bride adorned for her husband. ³ And I heard a loud voice from heaven saying, "Behold, the tabernacle of God is with men, and He will dwell with them, and they shall be His people. God Himself will be with them and be their God.
Revelation 21:1-3

Stay focused and encouraged because one-day things will go back to the way God originally intended it to be. He will dwell with us at the end of time, and we are His people, and He is our God!

What will you do differently if you were told the world is coming to an end in another month? Write your thoughts down, meditate on them and ask the Lord to help you live each day as if it were the end.

Your thought:

_____
_____
_____
_____
_____
_____

The best is yet to come . . .

> May God bless you and increase you as you grow in Him. If this has blessed you please write to us.
>
> Chosen Remnant Christian Ministries
> P.O. Box 800
> Powder Springs, GA 30127
> E-mail; Chosenremnant@gmail.com
> Website: www.chosenremnant.org
>
> All scriptures are from the New King James Version of the Bible unless otherwise stated.

www.ingramcontent.com/pod-product-compliance
Lightning Source LLC
Chambersburg PA
CBHW071457070426
42452CB00040B/1551